CAMBRIDGE LIBRARY COLLECTION

Books of enduring scholarly value

Egyptology

The large-scale scientific investigation of Egyptian antiquities by Western scholars began as an unintended consequence of Napoleon's invasion of Egypt during which, in 1799, the Rosetta Stone was discovered. The military expedition was accompanied by French scholars, whose reports prompted a wave of enthusiasm that swept across Europe and North America resulting in the Egyptian Revival style in art and architecture. Increasing numbers of tourists visited Egypt, eager to see the marvels being revealed by archaeological excavation. Writers and booksellers responded to this growing interest with publications ranging from technical site reports to tourist guidebooks and from children's histories to theories identifying the pyramids as repositories of esoteric knowledge. This series reissues a wide selection of such books. They reveal the gradual change from the 'tomb-robbing' approach of early excavators to the highly organised and systematic approach of Flinders Petrie, the 'father of Egyptology', and include early accounts of the decipherment of the hieroglyphic script.

The Religion of Ancient Egypt

A pioneering Egyptologist, Sir William Matthew Flinders Petrie (1853–1942) excavated over fifty sites and trained a generation of archaeologists. In this concise 1912 publication, aimed at non-specialists, Petrie discusses the key aspects of ancient Egyptian religion and the philosophies that underpinned it. Beginning with an explanation of the ancient conception of deities, the text explores the various types of god in the Egyptian pantheon and the ancient theory of the afterlife. It also gives due attention to such structures of belief as ritual, priesthood and scripture. The book ends with an examination of the ways in which ancient Egyptian religion spread through the ancient world and how Egyptian ideas were reused and transformed by later religions, including Christianity. Petrie wrote prolifically throughout his long career, and a great many of his other publications – for both specialists and non-specialists – are also reissued in this series.

T0352295

Cambridge University Press has long been a pioneer in the reissuing of out-of-print titles from its own backlist, producing digital reprints of books that are still sought after by scholars and students but could not be reprinted economically using traditional technology. The Cambridge Library Collection extends this activity to a wider range of books which are still of importance to researchers and professionals, either for the source material they contain, or as landmarks in the history of their academic discipline.

Drawing from the world-renowned collections in the Cambridge University Library and other partner libraries, and guided by the advice of experts in each subject area, Cambridge University Press is using state-of-the-art scanning machines in its own Printing House to capture the content of each book selected for inclusion. The files are processed to give a consistently clear, crisp image, and the books finished to the high quality standard for which the Press is recognised around the world. The latest print-on-demand technology ensures that the books will remain available indefinitely, and that orders for single or multiple copies can quickly be supplied.

The Cambridge Library Collection brings back to life books of enduring scholarly value (including out-of-copyright works originally issued by other publishers) across a wide range of disciplines in the humanities and social sciences and in science and technology.

The Religion of
Ancient Egypt

W.M. Flinders Petrie

CAMBRIDGE
UNIVERSITY PRESS

CAMBRIDGE
UNIVERSITY PRESS

University Printing House, Cambridge, CB2 8BS, United Kingdom

Published in the United States of America by Cambridge University Press, New York

Cambridge University Press is part of the University of Cambridge.
It furthers the University's mission by disseminating knowledge in the pursuit of
education, learning and research at the highest international levels of excellence.

www.cambridge.org
Information on this title: www.cambridge.org/9781108065788

© in this compilation Cambridge University Press 2013

This edition first published 1912
This digitally printed version 2013

ISBN 978-1-108-06578-8 Paperback

This book reproduces the text of the original edition. The content and language reflect
the beliefs, practices and terminology of their time, and have not been updated.

Cambridge University Press wishes to make clear that the book, unless originally published
by Cambridge, is not being republished by, in association or collaboration with, or
with the endorsement or approval of, the original publisher or its successors in title.

Religions Ancient and Modern

THE RELIGION OF ANCIENT EGYPT

HORUS   ISIS   OSIRIS

PTAH-SOKAR. BAST.   BES.

EGYPTIAN GODS. PETRIE COLLECTION

THE RELIGION OF
ANCIENT EGYPT

By

W. M. FLINDERS PETRIE

D.C.L., LL.D., LIT.D., PH.D., F.R.S., F.B.A., F.S.A. SCOT.
EDWARDS PROFESSOR OF EGYPTOLOGY,
UNIVERSITY COLLEGE, LONDON

LONDON
CONSTABLE & COMPANY LTD
10 ORANGE STREET LEICESTER SQUARE
1912

CONTENTS

PRINCIPAL WORKS ON EGYPTIAN RELIGION

LANZONE. — *Dizionario di Mitologia Egizia*, 1881-86. 1312 pp., 408 pls. About £4 second hand. (The indispensable storehouse of facts and references.)

WIEDEMANN. — *Religion of the Ancient Egyptians*, 1897. 307 pp, 73 figs. 12s.6d. (The best general view of the subject.)

WIEDEMANN.—Article in supplement to *Hastings's Dictionary of the Bible*. (Excellent outline.)

WIEDEMANN.—*Ancient Egyptian Doctrine of Immortality*, 1895. 71 pp., 21 figs., 2 pls. 3s.

MASPERO.—*Dawn of Civilisation*, see pp. 81-222, 1894. 25s. (A popular outline by a master.)

MASPERO.—*Études de Mythologie*, 1893, 895 pp.

MASPERO. — *Inscriptions des Pyramides de Saqqara*, 1894. 456 pp., 9 pl.

RENOUF.—*Book of the Dead*, 1893-1902. 308 pp., 53 pl. £2. (The standard translation with the illustrations.)

BUDGE.—*Gods of the Egyptians*, 1904. 908 pp., 131 figs., 98 pls. £3, 3s. (Useful repertory, but illustrations not exact.)

SAYCE.—*Religions of Ancient Egypt and Babylonia*, 1902. 509 pp. 7s. 6d. (Useful for comparative view.)

PETRIE.—*Religion and Conscience in Ancient Egypt*, 1898. 176 pp. 2s. 6d. (A study of the nature of conscience, and the tribal aspect of religion.)

THE RELIGION OF ANCIENT EGYPT

CHAPTER I

THE NATURE OF GODS

BEFORE dealing with the special varieties of the Egyptians' belief in gods, it is best to try to avoid a misunderstanding of their whole conception of the supernatural. The term god has come to tacitly imply to our minds such a highly special-ised group of attributes, that we can hardly throw our ideas back into the more remote conceptions to which we also attach the same name. It is un-fortunate that every other word for supernatural intelligences has become debased, so that we can-not well speak of demons, devils, ghosts, or fairies without implying a noxious or a trifling meaning, quite unsuited to the ancient deities that were so beneficent and powerful. If then we use the word god for such conceptions, it must always

A   I

be with the reservation that the word has now a very different meaning from what it had to ancient minds.

To the Egyptian the gods might be mortal; even Ra, the sun-god, is said to have grown old and feeble, Osiris was slain, and Orion, the great hunter of the heavens, killed and ate the gods. The mortality of gods has been dwelt on by Dr. Frazer (*Golden Bough*), and the many instances of tombs of gods, and of the slaying of the deified man who was worshipped, all show that immortality was not a divine attribute. Nor was there any doubt that they might suffer while alive; one myth tells how Ra, as he walked on earth, was bitten by a magic serpent and suffered torments. The gods were also supposed to share in a life like that of man, not only in Egypt but in most ancient lands. Offerings of food and drink were constantly supplied to them, in Egypt laid upon the altars, in other lands burnt for a sweet savour. At Thebes the divine wife of the god, or high priestess, was the head of the harem of concubines of the god; and similarly in Babylonia the chamber of the god with the golden couch could only be visited by the priestess who slept there for oracular responses. The Egyptian gods could not be cognisant of what passed on earth without being informed, nor could they reveal their will at a distant place except by sending a messenger; they were as limited as the Greek gods who required the aid of Iris to communicate one with another or with mankind. The gods, therefore, have no divine superiority to man in conditions or limitations; they can only be described as pre-existent, acting intelligences, with scarcely greater powers than man might hope to gain by magic or witchcraft of his own. This conception explains how easily the divine merged into the human in Greek theology, and how frequently divine ancestors occurred in family histories. (By the word 'theology' is designated the knowledge about gods.)

There are in ancient theologies very different classes of gods. Some races, as the modern Hindu, revel in a profusion of gods and godlings, which are continually being increased. Others, as the Turanians, whether Sumerian Babylonians, modern Siberians, or Chinese, do not adopt the worship of great gods, but deal with a host of animistic spirits, ghosts, devils, or whatever we may call them; and Shamanism or witchcraft is their system for conciliating such adversaries. But all our knowledge of the early positions and nature of great gods shows them to stand on an

3

entirely different footing to these varied spirits. Were the conception of a god only an evolution from such spirit worship we should find the worship of many gods preceding the worship of one god, polytheism would precede monotheism in each tribe or race. What we actually find is the contrary of this, monotheism is the first stage traceable in theology. Hence we must rather look on the theologic conception of the Aryan and Semitic races as quite apart from the demon-worship of the Turanians. Indeed the Chinese seem to have a mental aversion to the conception of a personal god, and to think either of the host of earth spirits and other demons, or else of the pantheistic abstraction of heaven.

Wherever we can trace back polytheism to its earliest stages we find that it results from combinations of monotheism. In Egypt even Osiris, Isis, and Horus (so familiar as a triad) are found at first as separate units in different places, Isis as a virgin goddess, and Horus as a self-existent god. Each city appears to have but one god belonging to it, to whom others were added. Similarly in Babylonia each great city had its supreme god; and the combinations of these, and their transformations in order to form them in

4

groups when their homes were politically united, show how essentially they were solitary deities at first.

Not only must we widely distinguish the demonology of races worshipping numerous earth spirits and demons, from the theology of races devoted to solitary great gods; but we must further distinguish the varying ideas of the latter class. Most of the theologic races have no objection to tolerating the worship of other gods side by side with that of their own local deity. It is in this way that the compound theologies built up the polytheism of Egypt and of Greece. But others of the theologic races have the conception of 'a jealous god,' who would not tolerate the presence of a rival. We cannot date this conception earlier than Mosaism, and this idea struggled hard against polytheistic toleration. This view acknowledges the reality of other gods, but ignores their claims. The still later view was that other gods were non-existent, a position started by the Hebrew prophets in contempt of idolatry, scarcely grasped by early Christianity, but triumphantly held by Islam.

We therefore have to deal with the following conceptions, which fall into two main groups,

5

that probably belong to different divisions of mankind:—

{ Animism.
{ Demonology.

⎧ Tribal Monotheism.
⎪ Combinations forming   ⎫ At any stage the unity of
⎨   tolerant Polytheism.   ⎬   different gods may be ac-
⎪ Jealous Monotheism.   ⎭   cepted as a *modus vivendi*
⎩ Sole Monotheism.   or as a philosophy.

All of these require mention here, as more or less of each principle, both of animism and monotheism, can be traced in the innumerable combinations found during the six thousand years of Egyptian religion: these combinations of beliefs being due to combinations of the races to which they belonged.

CHAPTER II

BEFORE we can understand what were the relations between man and the gods we must first notice the conceptions of the nature of man. In the prehistoric days of Egypt the position and direction of the body was always the same in every burial, offerings of food and drink were placed by it, figures of servants, furniture, even games, were included in the grave. It must be concluded therefore that it was a belief in immortality which gave rise to such a detailed ritual of the dead, though we have no written evidence upon this.

So soon as we reach the age of documents we find on tombstones that the person is denoted by the *khu* between the arms of the *ka*. From later writings it is seen that the *khu* is applied to a spirit of man; while the *ka* is not the body but the activities of sense and perception. Thus, in the earliest age of documents, two entities were believed to vitalise the body.

The *ka* is more frequently named than any other part, as all funeral offerings were made for the *ka*. It is said that if opportunities of satisfaction in life were missed it is grievous to the *ka*, and that the *ka* must not be annoyed needlessly; hence it was more than perception, and it included all that we might call consciousness. Perhaps we may grasp it best as the 'self,' with the same variety of meaning that we have in our own word. The *ka* was represented as a human being following after the man; it was born at the same time as the man, but it persisted after death and lived in and about the tomb. It could act and visit other *kas* after death, but it could not resist the least touch of physical force. It was always represented by two upraised arms, the acting parts of the person. Beside the *ka* of man, all objects likewise had their *kas*, which were comparable to the human *ka*, and among these the *ka* lived. This view leads closely to the world of ideas permeating the material world in later philosophy.

The *khu* is figured as a crested bird, which has the meaning of 'glorious' or 'shining' in ordinary use   It refers to a less material conception than

8

the *ka*, and may be called the intelligence or spirit.

The *khat* is the material body of man which was the vehicle of the *ka*, and inhabited by the *khu*.

The *ba* belongs to a different pneumatology to that just noticed. It is the soul apart from the body, figured as a human-headed bird. The concept probably arose from the white owls, with round heads and very human expressions, which frequent the tombs, flying noiselessly to and fro. The *ba* required food and drink, which were provided for it by the goddess of the cemetery. It thus overlaps the scope of the *ka*, and probably belongs to a different race to that which defined the *ka*.

The *sahu* or mummy is associated particularly with the *ba*; and the *ba* bird is often shown as resting on the mummy or seeking to re-enter it.

The *khaybet* was the shadow of a man; the importance of the shadow in early ideas is well known.

The *sekhem* was the force or ruling power of man, but is rarely mentioned.

The *ab* is the will and intentions, symbolised by the heart; often used in phrases, such as a man being 'in the heart of his lord,' 'wideness of heart' for satisfaction, 'washing of the heart' for giving vent to temper.

The *hati* is the physical heart, the 'chief' organ of the body, also used metaphorically.

The *ran* is the name which was essential to man, as also to inanimate things. Without a name nothing really existed. The knowledge of the name gave power over its owner; a great myth turns on Isis obtaining the name of Ra by stratagem, and thus getting the two eyes of Ra —the sun and moon—for her son Horus. Both in ancient and modern races the knowledge of the real name of a man is carefully guarded, and often secondary names are used for secular purposes. It was usual for Egyptians to have a 'great name' and a 'little name'; the great name is often compounded with that of a god or a king, and was very probably reserved for religious purposes, as it is only found on religious and funerary monuments.

We must not suppose by any means that all of these parts of the person were equally important, or were believed in simultaneously. The *ka, khu,* and *khat* seem to form one group; the *ba* and *sahu* belong to another; the *ab, hati,* and *sekhem* are hardly more than metaphors, such as we commonly use; the *khaybet* is a later idea which probably belongs to the system of animism and witchcraft, where the shadow gave a hold upon the man. The *ran*, name, belongs partly to the same system, but also is the germ of the later philosophy of idea.

The purpose of religion to the Egyptian was to secure the favour of the god. There is but little trace of negative prayer to avert evils or deprecate evil influences, but rather of positive prayer for concrete favours. On the part of kings this is usually of the Jacob type, offering to provide temples and services to the god in return for material prosperity. The Egyptian was essentially self-satisfied, he had no confession to make of sin or wrong, and had no thought of pardon. In the judgment he boldly averred that he was free of the forty-two sins that might prevent his entry into the kingdom of Osiris. If he failed to establish his innocence in the weighing of his heart, there was no other plea, but he was consumed by fire and by a hippopotamus, and no hope remained for him.

CHAPTER III

THE various beliefs of the Egyptians regarding the future life are so distinct from each other and so incompatible, that they may be classified into groups more readily than the theology; thus they serve to indicate the varied sources of the religion.

The most simple form of belief was that of the continued existence of the soul in the tomb and about the cemetery. In Upper Egypt at present a hole is left at the top of the tomb chamber; and I have seen a woman remove the covering of the hole, and talk down to her deceased husband. Also funeral offerings of food and drink, and even beds, are still placed in the tombs. A similar feeling, without any precise beliefs, doubtless prompted the earlier forms of provision for the dead. The soul wandered around the tomb seeking sustenance, and was fed by the

12

goddess who dwelt in the thick sycomore trees that overshadowed the cemetery. She is represented as pouring out drink for the *ba* and holding a tray of cakes for it to feed upon. In the grave we find this belief shown by the jars of water, wine, and perhaps other liquids, the stores of corn, the geese, haunches and heads of oxen, the cakes, and dates, and pomegranates which were laid by the dead. In an early king's tomb there might be many rooms full of these offerings. There were also the weapons for defence and for the chase, the toilet objects, the stores of clothing, the draughtsmen, and even the literature of papyri buried with the dead. The later form of this system was the representation of all these offerings in sculpture and drawing in the tomb. This modification probably belongs to the belief in the *ka*, which could be supported by the *ka* of the food and use the *ka* of the various objects, the figures of the objects being supposed to provide the *kas* of them. This system is entirely complete in itself, and does not presuppose or require any theologic connection. It might well belong to an age of simple animism, and be a survival of that in later times.

The greatest theologic system was that of the kingdom of Osiris. This was a counterpart of the earthly life, but was reserved for the worthy. All the dead belonged to Osiris and were brought before him for judgment. The protest of being innocent of the forty-two sins was made, and then the heart was weighed against truth, symbolised by the ostrich feather, the emblem of the goddess of truth. From this feather, the emblem of lightness, being placed against the heart in weighing, it seems that sins were considered to weigh down the heart, and its lightness required to be proved. Thoth, the god who recorded the weighing, then stated that the soul left the judgment hall true of voice with his heart and members restored to him, and that he should follow Osiris in his kingdom. This kingdom of Osiris was at first thought of as being in the marshlands of the delta; when these became familiar it was transferred to Syria, and finally to the north-east of the sky, where the Milky Way became the heavenly Nile. The main occupation in this kingdom was agriculture, as on earth; the souls ploughed the land, sowed the corn, and reaped the harvest of heavenly maize, taller and fatter than any of this world. In this land they rowed on the heavenly streams, they sat in shady arbours, and played the games which they had loved. But the cultivation was a toil, and therefore it was to be done by numerous serfs. In the beginning of the monarchy it seems that the servants of the king were all buried around him to serve him in the future; from the second to the twelfth dynasty we lose sight of this idea, and then we find slave figures buried in the tombs. These figures were provided with the hoe for tilling the soil, the pick for breaking the clods, a basket for carrying the earth, a pot for watering the crops, and they were inscribed with an order to respond for their master when he was called on to work in the fields. In the eighteenth dynasty the figures sometimes have actual tool models buried with them; but usually the tools are in relief or painted on the figure. This idea continued until the less material view of the future life arose in Greek times; then the deceased man was said to have 'gone to Osiris' in such a year of his age, but no slave figures were laid with him. This view of the future is complete in itself, and is appropriately provided for in the

A third view of the future life belongs to an entirely different theologic system, that of the progress of the sun-god Ra. According to this the soul went to join the setting sun in the west, and prayed to be allowed to enter the boat of the sun in the company of the gods; thus it would be taken along in everlasting light, and saved from the terrors and demons of the night over which the sun triumphed. No occupations were predicated of this future; simply to rest in the divine company was the entire purpose, and the successful repelling of the powers of darkness in each hour of the night by means of spells was the only activity. To provide for the solar journey a model boat was placed in the tomb with the figures of boatmen, to enable the dead to sail with the sun, or to reach the solar bark. This view of the future implied a journey to the west, and hence came the belief in the soul setting out to cross the desert westward. We find also an early god of the dead, Khent-amenti, 'he who is in the west,' probably arising from this same view. This god was later identified with Osiris when the fusion of the two theories of the soul arose. At Abydos Khent-amenti only is named at first, and Osiris does not appear until later times, though that cemetery came to be regarded as specially dedicated to Osiris.

Now in all these views that we have named there is no occasion for preserving the body. It is the *ba* that is fed in the cemetery, not the body. It is an immaterial body that takes part in the kingdom of Osiris, in the sky. It is an immaterial body that can accompany the gods in the boat of the sun. There is so far no call to conserve the body by the peculiar mummification which first appears in the early dynasties. The dismemberment of the bones, and removal of the flesh, which was customary in the prehistoric times, and survived down to the fifth dynasty, would accord with any of these theories, all of which were probably predynastic. But the careful mummifying of the body became customary only in the third or fourth dynasty, and is therefore later than the theories that we have noticed. The idea of thus preserving the body seems to look forward to some later revival of it on earth, rather than to a personal life immediately after death. The funeral accompaniment of this view was the abundance of amulets placed on various parts of the body to preserve it. A few amulets are found worn on a necklace or bracelet in early times; but the full development of the amulet system was in the twenty-sixth to thirtieth dynasties.

We have tried to disentangle the diverse types of belief, by seeing what is incompatible between them. But in practice we find every form of mixture of these views in most ages. In the pre-

historic times the preservation of the bones, but
not of the flesh, was constant; and food offerings
show that at least the theory of the soul wander-
ing in the cemetery was familiar. Probably the
Osiris theory is also of the later prehistoric times,
as the myth of Osiris is certainly older than the
dynasties. The Ra worship was associated specially with Heliopolis, and may have given rise to
the union with Ra also before the dynasties, when
Heliopolis was probably a capital of the kings of
Lower Egypt. The boats figured on the prehistoric tomb at Hierakonpolis bear this out. In
the first dynasty there is no mummy known,
funeral offerings abound, and the *khu* and *ka* are
named. Our documents do not give any evidence,
then, of the Osiris and Ra theories. In the
pyramid period the king was called the Osiris,
and this view is the leading one in the Pyramid
inscriptions, yet the Ra theory is also incom-
patibly present; the body is mummified; but
funeral offerings of food seem to have much
diminished. In the eighteenth and nineteenth
dynasties the Ra theory gained ground greatly
over the Osirian; and the basis of all the views
of the future is almost entirely the union with
Ra during the night and day. The mummy and
amulet theory was not dominant; but the funeral

offerings somewhat increased. The twenty-sixth dynasty almost dropped the Ra theory; the Osirian kingdom and its population of slave figures is the most familiar view, and the preservation of the body by amulets was essential. Offerings of food rarely appear in these later times. This dominance of Osiris leads on to the anthropomorphic worship, which interacts on the growth of Christianity as we shall see further. Lastly, when all the theologic views of the future had perished, the oldest idea of all, food, drink, and rest for the dead, has still kept its hold upon the feelings of the people in spite of the teachings of Islam.

CHAPTER IV

ANIMAL WORSHIP

THE worship of animals has been known in many countries; but in Egypt it was maintained to a later pitch of civilisation than elsewhere, and the mixture of such a primitive system with more elevated beliefs seemed as strange to the Greek as it does to us. The original motive was a kinship of animals with man, much like that underlying the system of totems. Each place or tribe had its sacred species that was linked with the tribe; the life of the species was carefully preserved, excepting in the one example selected for worship, which after a given time was killed and sacramentally eaten by the tribe. This was certainly the case with the bull at Memphis and the ram at Thebes. That it was the whole species that was sacred, at one place or another, is shown by the penalties for killing any animal of the species, by the wholesale burial and even mummifying of every example, and by the plural form of

20

the names of the gods later connected with the animals, *Heru*, hawks, *Khnumu*, rams, etc.

In the prehistoric times the serpent was sacred; figures of the coiled serpent were hung up in the house and worn as an amulet; similarly in historic times a figure of the agathodemon serpent was placed in a temple of Amenhotep III at Benha. In the first dynasty the serpent was figured in pottery, as a fender round the hearth. The hawk also appears in many predynastic figures, large and small, both worn on the person and carried as standards. The lion is found both in life-size temple figures, lesser objects of worship, and personal amulets. The scorpion was similarly honoured in the prehistoric ages.

It is difficult to separate now between animals which were worshipped quite independently, and those which were associated as emblems of anthropomorphic gods. Probably we shall be right in regarding both classes of animals as having been sacred at a remote time, and the connection with the human form as being subsequent. The ideas connected with the animals were those of their most prominent characteristics; hence it appears that it was for the sake of the character that each animal was worshipped, and not because of any fortuitous association with a tribe.

The baboon was regarded as the emblem of Tahuti, the god of wisdom; the serious expression and human ways of the large baboons are an obvious cause for their being regarded as the wisest of animals. Tahuti is represented as a baboon from the first dynasty down to late times; and four baboons were sacred in his temple at Hermopolis. These four baboons were often portrayed as adoring the sun; this idea is due to their habit of chattering at sunrise.

The lioness appears in the compound figures of the goddesses Sekhet, Bast, Mahes, and Tefnut. In the form of Sekhet the lioness is the destructive power of Ra, the sun: it is Sekhet who, in the legend, destroys mankind from Herakleopolis to Heliopolis at the bidding of Ra. The other lioness goddesses are probably likewise destructive or hunting deities. The lesser *felidae* also appear; the *cheetah* and *serval* are sacred to Hathor in Sinai; the small cats are sacred to Bast, especially at Speos Artemidos and Bubastis.

The bull was sacred in many places, and his worship underlay that of the human gods, who were said to be incarnated in him. The idea is that of the fighting power, as when the king is figured as a bull trampling on his enemies, and the reproductive power, as in the title of the self-renewing gods, 'bull of his mother.' The most renowned was the *Hapi* or Apis bull of Memphis, in whom Ptah was said to be incarnate, and who was Osirified and became the Osir-hapi. This appears to have originated the great Ptolemaic god Serapis, as certainly the mausoleum of the bulls was the Serapeum of the Greeks. Another bull of a more massive breed was the *Ur-mer* or Mnevis of Heliopolis, in whom Ra was incarnate. A third bull was *Bakh* or Bakis of Hermonthis the incarnation of Mentu. And a fourth bull, *Ka-nub* or Kanobos, was worshipped at the city of that name. The cow was identified with Hathor, who appears with cow's ears and horns, and who is probably the cow-goddess Ashtaroth or Istar of Asia. Isis, as identified with Hathor, is also joined in this connection.

The ram was also worshipped as a procreative god; at Mendes in the Delta identified with Osiris, at Herakleopolis identified with Hershefi, at Thebes as Amon, and at the cataract as Khnumu the creator. The association of the ram with Amon was strongly held by the Ethiopians; and in the Greek tale of Nektanebo, the last Pharaoh, having by magic visited Olympias and become the father of Alexander, he came as the incarnation of Amon wearing the ram's skin.

The hippopotamus was the goddess Ta-urt, 'the great one,' the patroness of pregnancy, who is never shown in any other form. Rarely this animal appears as the emblem of the god Set.

The jackal haunted the cemeteries on the edge of the desert, and so came to be taken as the guardian of the dead, and identified with Anubis, the god of departing souls. Another aspect of the jackal was as the maker of tracks in the desert; the jackal paths are the best guides to practicable courses, avoiding the valleys and precipices, and so the animal was known as Up-uat, 'the opener of ways,' who showed the way for the dead across the western desert. Species of dogs seem to have been held sacred and mummified on merely the general ground of confusion with the jackal. The ichneumon and the shrewmouse were also held sacred, though not identified with a human god.

The hawk was the principal sacred bird, and was identified with Horus and Ra, the sun-god. It was mainly worshipped at Edfu and Hierakonpolis. The souls of kings were supposed to fly up to heaven in the form of hawks, perhaps due to the kingship originating in the hawk district in Upper Egypt. Seker, the god of the dead, appears as a mummified hawk, and on his boat are many small hawks, perhaps the souls of kings who have joined him. The mummy hawk is also Sopdu, the god of the east.

The vulture was the emblem of maternity, as being supposed to care especially for her young. Hence she is identified with Mut, the mother goddess of Thebes. The queen-mothers have vulture head-dresses; the vulture is shown hovering over kings to protect them, and a row of spread-out vultures are figured on the roofs of the tomb passages to protect the soul. The ibis was identified with Tahuti, the god of Hermopolis. The goose is connected with Amon of Thebes. The swallow was also sacred.

The crocodile was worshipped especially in the Fayum, where it frequented the marshy levels of the great lake, and Strabo's description of the feeding of the sacred crocodile there is familiar. It was also worshipped at Onuphis; and at Nubti or Ombos it was identified with Set, and held sacred. Beside the name of Sebek or Soukhos in Fayum, it was there identified with Osiris as the western god of the dead. The frog was an emblem of the goddess Heqt, but was not worshipped.

The cobra serpent was sacred from the earliest times to the present day. It was never identified with any of the great deities, but three goddesses appear in serpent form: Uazet, the Delta goddess of Buto; Mert-seger, 'the lover of silence,' the goddess of the Theban necropolis; and Rannut, the harvest goddess. The memory of great pythons of the prehistoric days appears in the serpent-necked monsters on the slate palettes at the beginning of the monarchy, and the immense serpent Apap of the underworld in the later mythology. The serpent has however been a popular object of worship apart from specific gods. We have already noted it on prehistoric amulets, and coiled round the hearths of the early dynasties. Serpents were mummified; and when we reach the full evidences of popular worship, in the terra-cotta figures and jewellery of later times, the serpent is very prominent. There were usually two represented together, one often with the head of Serapis, the other of Isis, so therefore male and female. Down to modern times a serpent is worshipped at Sheykh Heridy, and miraculous cures attributed to it (S.R.E.B. 213).

Various fishes were sacred, as the Oxyrhynkhos, Phagros, Lepidotos, Latos, and others; but they were not identified with gods, and we do not know of their being worshipped. The scorpion was the emblem of the goddess Selk, and is found in prehistoric amulets; but it is not known to have been adored, and most usually it represents evil, where Horus is shown overcoming noxious creatures.

It will be observed that nearly all of the animals which were worshipped had qualities for which they were noted, and in connection with which they were venerated. If the animal worship were due to totemism, or a sense of animal brotherhood in certain tribes, we must also assume that that was due to these qualities of the animal; whereas totemism in other countries does not seem to be due to veneration of special qualities of the animals. It is therefore more likely that the animal worship simply arose from the nature of the animals, and not from any true totemism, although each animal came to be associated with the worship of a particular tribe or district.

CHAPTER V

THE GROUPS OF GODS.   ANIMAL-HEADED GODS

IN a country which has been subjected to so many inflows of various peoples as in Egypt, it is to be expected that there would be a great diversity of deities and a complex and inconsistent theology. To discriminate the principal classes of conceptions of gods is the first step toward understanding the growth of the systems. The broad division of animal gods and human gods is obvious; and the mixed type of human figures with animal heads is clearly an adaptation of the animal gods to the later conceptions of a human god. Another valuable separator lies in the compound names of gods. It is impossible to suppose a people uniting two gods, both of which belonged to them aboriginally; there would be no reason for two similar gods in a single system, and we never hear in classical mythology of Hermes-Apollo or Pallas-Artemis, while Zeus is compounded with half of the barbarian gods of Asia. So in Egypt, when

28

we find such compounds as Amon-Ra, or Ptah-Sokar-Osiris, we have the certainty that each name in the compound is derived from a different race, and that a unifying operation has taken place on gods that belonged to entirely different sources.

We must beware of reading our modern ideas into the ancient views. As we noticed in the first chapter, each tribe or locality seems to have had but one god originally; certainly the more remote our view, the more separate are the gods. Hence to the people of any one district 'the god' was a distinctive name for their own god; and it would have seemed as strange to discriminate him from the surrounding gods, as it would to a Christian in Europe if he specified that he did not mean Allah or Siva or Heaven when he speaks of God. Hence we find generic descriptions used in place of the god's name, as 'lord of heaven,' or 'mistress of turquoise,' while it is certain that specific gods as Osiris or Hathor are in view. A generic name 'god' or 'the god' no more implies that the Egyptians recognised a unity of all the gods, than 'god' in the Old Testament implies that Yahvah was one with Chemosh and Baal. The simplicity of the term only shows that no other object of adoration was in view.

We have already noticed the purely animal gods; following on these we now shall describe those which were combined with a human form, then those which are purely human in their character, next those which are nature gods, and lastly those which are of an abstract character. The gods which belonged to peoples who did not conquer or occupy Egypt must be ranked as foreign gods.

Animal-Headed Gods.—Beside the worship of species of animals, which we have noticed in the last chapter, certain animals were combined with the human form. It was always the head of the animal which was united to a human body; the only converse instance of a human head on an animal body—the sphinxes—represented the king and not a god. Possibly the combination arose from priests wearing the heads of animals when personating the god, as the high priest wore the ram's skin when personating Amon. But when we notice the frequent combinations and love of symbolism, shown upon the early carvings, the union of the ancient sacred animal with the human form is quite in keeping with the views and feelings of the primitive Egyptians. Many of these composite gods never emerged from the animal connection, and these we must regard as belonging to the earlier stage of theology.

Seker was a Memphite god of the dead, independent of the worship of Osiris and of Ptah, for he was combined with them as Ptah-Seker-Osiris; as he maintained a place there in the face of the great worship of Ptah, he was probably an older god, and this is indicated by his having an entirely animal form down to a late date. The sacred bark of Seker bore his figure as that of a mummified hawk; and along the boat is a row of hawks which probably are the spirits of deceased kings who have joined Seker in his journey to the world of the dead. As there are often two allied forms of the same root, one written with k and the other with g,[1] it seems probable that Seker, the funeral god of Memphis, is allied to

Mert Seger (lover of silence). She was the funeral god of Thebes, and was usually figured as a serpent. From being only known in animal form, and unconnected with any of the elaborated theology, it seems that we have in this goddess a primitive deity of the dead. It appears, then, that the gods of the great cemeteries were known

---

[1] For instance the words *sek*, to move; *seg*, to go; *sek*, to destroy; *sega*, to break; *kauy*, cow; *gaua*, ox; *keba* and *geba*, sky, etc.

as Silence and the Lover of Silence, and both come down from the age of animal deities. Seker became in late times changed into a hawk-headed human figure.

Two important deities of early times were **Nekhebt**, the vulture goddess of the southern kingdom, centred at Hierakonpolis, and **Uazet**, the serpent goddess of the northern kingdom, centred at Buto. These appear in all ages as the emblems of the two kingdoms, frequently as supporters on either side of the royal names; in later times they appear as human goddesses crowning the king.

Khnumu, the creator, was the great god of the cataract. He is shown as making man upon the potter's wheel; and in a tale he is said to frame a woman. He must belong to a different source from that of Ptah or Ra, and was the creative principle in the period of animal gods, as he is almost always shown with the head of a ram. He was popular down to late times, where amulets of his figure are often found.

Tahuti or **Thōth** was the god of writing and learning, and was the chief deity of Hermopolis. He almost always has the head of an ibis, the bird sacred to him. The baboon is also a frequent emblem of his, but he is never figured with the

32

baboon head. The ibis appears standing upon a shrine as early as on a tablet of Mena; Thŏth is the constant recorder in scenes of the judgment, and he appears down to Roman times as the patron of scribes. The eighteenth dynasty of kings incorporated his name as Thŏthmes, 'born of Thŏth,' owing to their Hermopolite origin.

Sekhmet is the lion goddess, who represents the fierceness of the sun's heat. She appears in the myth of the destruction of mankind as slaughtering the enemies of Ra. Her only form is that with the head of a lioness. But she blends imperceptibly with

Bastet, who has the head of a cat. She was the goddess of Pa-bast or Bubastis, and in her honour immense festivals were there held. Her name is found in the beginning of the pyramid times; but her main period of popularity was that of the Shishaks who ruled from Bubastis, and in the later times images of her were very frequent as amulets. It is possible from the name that this feline goddess, whose foreign origin is acknowledged, was the female form of the god Bes, who is dressed in a lion's skin, and also came in from the east (see chap. ix).

Mentu was the hawk-god of Erment south of Thebes, who became in the eighteenth to

C   33

twentieth dynasties especially the god of war. He appears with the hawk head, or sometimes as a hawk-headed sphinx; and he became confused with Ra and with Amon.

Sebek is figured as a man with the crocodile's head; but he has no theologic importance, and always remained the local god of certain districts.

Heqt, the goddess symbolised by the frog, was the patron of birth, and assisted in the infancy of the kings. She was a popular and general deity not mainly associated with particular places.

Hershefi was the ram-headed god of Herakleopolis, but is never found outside of that region.

We now come to three animal-headed gods who became associated with the great Osiride group of human gods. **Set** or **Setesh** was the god of the prehistoric inhabitants before the coming in of Horus. He is always shown with the head of a fabulous animal, having upright square ears and a long nose. When in entirely animal form he has a long upright tail. The dog-like animal is the earliest type, as in the second dynasty; but later the human form with animal head prevailed. His worship underwent great fluctuations. At first he was the great god of all Egypt; but his worshippers were gradually driven out by the followers of Horus, as described in a semi-mythical history. Then he appears strongly in the second dynasty, the last king of which united the worship of Set and Horus. In the early formulae for the dead he is honoured equally with Horus. After suppression he appears in favour in the early eighteenth dynasty; and even gave the name to Sety I and II of the nineteenth dynasty. His part in the Osiris myth will be noted below.

Anpu or **Anubis** was originally the jackal guardian of the cemetery, and the leader of the dead in the other world. Nearly all the early funeral formulae mention Anpu on his hill, or Anpu lord of the underworld. As the patron of the dead he naturally took a place in the myth of Osiris, the god of the dead, and appears as leading the soul into the judgment of Osiris.

Horus was the hawk-god of Upper Egypt, especially of Edfu and Hierakonpolis. Though originally an independent god, and even keeping apart as Hor-ur, 'Horus the elder,' throughout later times, yet he was early mingled with the Osiris myth, probably as the ejector of Set who was also the enemy of Osiris. He is sometimes entirely in hawk form; more usually with a hawk's head, and in later times he appears as the infant son of Isis entirely human in form.

35

His special function is that of overcoming evil; in the earliest days the conqueror of Set, later as the subduer of noxious animals, figured on a very popular amulet, and lastly, in Roman times, as a hawk-headed warrior on horseback slaying a dragon, thus passing into the type of St. George. He also became mingled with early Christian ideas; and the lock of hair of Horus attached to the cross originated the *chi rho* monogram of Christ.

We have now passed briefly over the principal gods which combined the animal and human forms. We see how the animal form is generally the older, and how it was apparently independent of the human form, which has been attached to it by a more anthropomorphic people. We see that all of these gods must be accredited to the second stratum, if not to the earliest formation, of religion in Egypt. And we must associate with this theology the cemetery theory of the soul which preceded that of the Osiris or Ra religions,

CHAPTER VI

THE HUMAN GODS

WE now turn to the deities which are always represented in human form, and never associated with animal figures; neither do they originate in a cosmic—or nature—worship, nor in abstract ideas. There are three divisions of this class, the Osiris family, the Amon family, and the goddess Neit.

Osiris (*Asar* or *Asir*) is the most familiar figure of the pantheon, but it is mainly on late sources that we have to depend for the myth; and his worship was so much adapted to harmonise with other ideas, that care is needed to trace his true position. The Osiride portions of the *Book of the Dead* are certainly very early, and precede the solar portions, though both views were already mingled in the pyramid texts. We cannot doubt but that the Osiris worship reaches back to the prehistoric age. In the earliest tombs offering to Anubis is named, for whom Osiris became substituted in the fifth and sixth dynasties. In the pyramid times we only find that kings are termed Osiris, having undergone their apotheosis at the *sed* festival; but in the eighteenth dynasty and onward every justified person was entitled the Osiris, as being united with the god. His worship was unknown at Abydos in the earlier temples, and is not mentioned at the cataracts; though in later times he became the leading deity of Abydos and of Philae. Thus in all directions the recognition of Osiris continued to increase; but, looking at the antiquity of his cult, we must recognise in this change the gradual triumph of a popular religion over a state religion which had been superimposed upon it. The earliest phase of Osirism that we can identify is in portions of the *Book of the Dead*. These assume the kingdom of Osiris, and a judgment preceding admission to the blessed future; the completely human character of Osiris and his family are implied, and there is no trace of animal or nature-worship belonging to him. How far the myth, as recorded in Roman times by Plutarch, can be traced to earlier and later sources is very uncertain. The main outlines, which may be primitive, are as follow. Osiris was a civilising king of Egypt, who was murdered by his brother Set and seventy-two conspirators. Isis, his wife, found the coffin of Osiris at Byblos in Syria and brought it to Egypt. Set then tore up the body of Osiris and scattered it. Isis sought the fragments, and built a shrine over each of them. Isis and Horus then attacked Set and drove him from Egypt, and finally down the Red Sea. In other aspects Osiris seems to have been a corn god, and the scattering of his body in Egypt is like the well-known division of the sacrifice to the corn god, and the burial of parts in separate fields to ensure their fertility.

How we are to analyse the formation of the early myths is suggested by the known changes of later times. When two tribes who worshipped different gods fought together and one overcame the other, the god of the conqueror is always considered to have overcome the god of the vanquished. The struggle of Horus and Set is expressly stated on the Temple of Edfu to have been a tribal war, in which the followers of Horus overcame those of Set, established garrisons and forges at various places down the Nile valley, and finally ousted the Set party from the whole land. We can hardly therefore avoid reading the history of the animosities of the gods as being the struggles of their worshippers

RELIGION OF ANCIENT EGYPT

If we try to trace the historic basis of the Osiris myth, we must take into account the early customs and ideas among which the myths arose. The cutting up of the body was the regular ritual of the prehistoric people, and (even as late as the fifth dynasty) the bones were separately treated, and even wrapped up separately when the body was reunited for burial. We must also notice the apotheosis festival of the king, which was probably his sacrificial death and union with the god, in the prehistoric age. The course of events which might have served as the basis for the Osiris myth may then have been somewhat as follows. Osiris was the god of a tribe which occupied a large part of Egypt. The kings of this tribe were sacrificed after thirty years' reign (like the killing of kings at fixed intervals elsewhere), and they thus became the Osiris himself. Their bodies were dismembered, as usual at that period, the flesh ceremonially eaten by the assembled people (as was done in prehistoric times), and the bones distributed among the various centres of the tribe, the head to Abydos, the neck, spine, limbs, etc., to various places, of which there were fourteen in all. The worshippers of Set broke in upon this people, stopped this worship, or killed Osiris, as was said, and established the dominion of their animal god. They were in turn attacked by the Isis worshippers, who joined the older population of the Osiris tribe, re-opened the shrines, and established Osiris worship again. The Set tribe returning in force attacked the Osiris tribe and scattered all the relics of the shrines in every part of the land. To re-establish their power, the Osiris and Isis tribes called in the worshippers of the hawk Horus, who were old enemies of the Set tribe, and with their help finally expelled the Set worshippers from the whole country. Such a history, somewhat mis-understood in a later age when the sacrifice of kings and anthropophagy was forgotten, would give the basis for nearly all the features of the Osiris myth as recorded in Roman times.

If we try to materialise this history more closely we see that the Osiris worshippers occu-pied both the Delta and Upper Egypt, and that fourteen important centres were recognised at the earliest time, which afterwards became the capitals of nomes, and were added to until they numbered forty-two divisions in later ages. Set was the god of the Asiatic invaders who broke in upon this civilisation; and about a quarter through the long ages of the prehistoric culture (perhaps 7500 B.C.) we find material evidences of considerable changes brought in from the Arabian or Semitic side. It may not be unlikely that this was the first triumph of Set. The Isis worshippers came from the Delta, where Isis was worshipped at Buto as a virgin goddess, apart from Osiris or Horus. These followers of Isis succeeded in helping the rest of the early Libyan inhabitants to resist the Set worship, and re-establish Osiris. The close of the prehistoric age is marked by a great decline in work and abilities, very likely due to more trouble from Asia, when Set scattered the relics of Osiris. Lastly, we cannot avoid seeing in the Horus triumph the conquest of Egypt by the dynastic race who came down from the district of Edfu and Hierakonpolis, the centres of Horus worship; and helped the older inhabitants to drive out the Asiatics. Nearly the same chain of events is seen in later times, when the Berber king Aahmes I helped the Egyptians to expel the Hyksos. If we can thus succeed in connecting the archaeology of the prehistoric age with the history preserved in the myths, it shows that Osiris must have been the national god as early as the beginning of prehistoric culture. His civilising mission may well have been the introduction of cultivation, at about 8000 B.C., into the Nile valley.

THE HUMAN GODS

The theology of Osiris was at first that of a god of those holy fields in which the souls of the dead enjoyed a future life. There was necessarily some selection to exclude the wicked from such happiness, and Osiris judged each soul whether it were worthy. This judgment became elaborated in detailed scenes, where Isis and Neb-hat stand behind Osiris who is on his throne, Anubis leads in the soul, the heart is placed in the balance, and Thōth stands to weigh it and to record the result. The occupations of the souls in this future we have noticed in chapter iii. The function of Osiris was therefore the reception and rule of the dead, and we never find him as a god of action or patronising any of the affairs of life.

Isis (*Aset* or *Isit*) became attached at a very early time to the Osiris worship; and appears in later myths as the sister and wife of Osiris. But she always remained on a very different plane to Osiris. Her worship and priesthood were far more popular than those of Osiris, persons were named after her much more often than after Osiris, and she appears far more usually in the activities of life. Her union in the Osiris myth by no means blotted out her independent position and importance as a deity, though it gave her

a far more widespread devotion. The union of
Horus with the myth, and the establishment of
Isis as the mother goddess, was the main mode
of her importance in later times. Isis as the
nursing mother is seldom shown until the twenty-
sixth dynasty; then the type continually became
more popular, until it outgrew all other religions
of the country. In the Roman times the mother
Isis not only received the devotion of all Egypt,
but her worship spread rapidly abroad, like that
of Mithra. It became the popular devotion
of Italy; and, after a change of name due
to the growth of Christianity, she has continued to receive the adoration of a large part
of Europe down to the present day as the
Madonna.

Nephthys (*Neb-hat*) was a shadowy double of
Isis; reputedly her sister, and always associated
with her, she seems to have no other function.
Her name, 'mistress of the palace,' suggests that
she was the consort of Osiris at the first, as a
necessary but passive complement in the system
of his kingdom. When the active Isis worship
entered into the renovation of Osiris, Nebhat
remained of nominal importance, but practically
ignored.

Horus (*Heru* or *Horu*) has a more complex

44

history than any other god. We cannot assign
the various stages of it with certainty, but we can
discriminate the following ideas. (*A*) There was
an elder or greater Horus, *Hor-ur* (or Aroeris of
the Greeks) who was credited with being the
brother of Osiris, older than Isis, Set, or Nephthys.
He was always in human form, and was the god
of Letopolis. This seems to have been the
primitive god of a tribe cognate to the Osiris
worshippers. What connection this god had
with the hawk we do not know; often Horus is
found written without the hawk, simply as *hr*,
with the meaning of 'upper' or 'above.' This
word generally has the determinative of sky, and
so means primitively the sky or one belonging to
the sky. It is at least possible that there was a
sky-god *her* at Letopolis, and likewise the hawk-
god was a sky-god *her* at Edfu, and hence the
mixture of the two deities. (*B*) The hawk-god of
the south, at Edfu and Hierakonpolis, became so
firmly embedded in the myth as the avenger of
Osiris, that we must accept the southern people
as the ejectors of the Set tribe. It is always the
hawk-headed Horus who wars against Set, and
attends on the enthroned Osiris. (*C*) The hawk
Horus became identified with the sun-god, and
hence came the winged solar disk as the emblem

of Horus of Edfu, and the title of Horus on the horizons (at rising and setting) Hor-em-akhti, Harmakhis of the Greeks. (*D*) Another aspect resulting from Horus being the 'sky' god, was that the sun and moon were his two eyes; hence he was Hor-merti, Horus of the two eyes, and the sacred eye of Horus (*uza*) became the most usual of all amulets. (*E*) Horus, as conqueror of Set, appears as the hawk standing on the sign of gold, *nub*; *nubti* was the title of Set, and thus Horus is shown trampling upon Set; this became a usual title of the kings. There are many less important forms of Horus, but the form which outgrew all others in popular estimation was (*F*) Hor-pe-khroti, Harpokrates of the Greeks, 'Horus the child.' As the son of Isis he constantly appears from the nineteenth dynasty onward. One of the earlier of these forms is that of the boy Horus standing upon crocodiles, and grasping scorpions and noxious animals in his hands. This type was a favourite amulet down to Ptolemaic times, and is often found carved in stone to be placed in a house, but was scarcely ever made in other materials or for suspension on the person. The form of the young Horus seated on an open lotus flower was also popular in the Greek times. But the infant Horus with his finger to his lips was the most popular form of all, sometimes alone, sometimes on his mother's lap. The finger, which pointed to his being a sucking child, was absurdly misunderstood by the Greeks as an emblem of silence. From the twenty-sixth dynasty down to late Roman times the infant Horus, or the young boy, was the most prominent subject on the temples, and the commonest figure in the homes of the people.

The other main group of human gods was Amon, Mut, and Khonsu of Thebes. **Amon** was the local god of Karnak, and owed his importance in Egypt to the political rise of his district. The Theban kingdom of the twelfth dynasty spread his fame, the great kings of the eighteenth and nineteenth dynasty ascribed their victories to Amon, his high priest became a political power which absorbed the state after the twentieth dynasty, and the importance of the god only ceased with the fall of his city. The original attributes and the origin of the name of Amon are unknown; but he became combined with Ra, the sun-god, and as Amon-Ra he was 'king of the gods,' and 'lord of the thrones of the world.' The supremacy of Amon was for some centuries an article of political faith, and many other gods were merged in him, and only survived as aspects of the great god of all. The queens were the high priestesses of the god, and he was the divine father of their children; the kings being only incarnations of Amon in their relation to the queens.

Mut, the great mother, was the goddess of Thebes, and hence the consort of Amon. She is often shown as leading and protecting the kings, and the queens appear in the character of this goddess. Little is known about her otherwise, and she disappears in the later theology.

Khonsu is a youthful god combined in the Theban system as the son of Amon and Mut. He is closely parallel to Thōth as being a god of time, as a moon god, and of science, 'the executor of plans.' A large temple was dedicated to him at Karnak, but otherwise he was not of religious importance.

Neit was a goddess of the Libyan people; but her worship was firmly implanted by them in Egypt. She was a goddess of hunting and of weaving, the two arts of a nomadic people. Her emblem was a distaff with two crossed arrows, and her name was written with a figure of a weaver's shuttle. She was adored in the first dynasty, when the name Merneit, 'loved by Neit,' occurs; and her priesthood was one of the most usual in the pyramid period. She was almost lost to sight during some thousands of years, but she became the state goddess of the twenty-sixth dynasty, when the Libyans set up their capital in her city of Sais. In later times she again disappears from customary religion.

CHAPTER VII

THE COSMIC GODS

THE gods which personify the sun and sky stand apart in their essential idea from those already described, although they were largely mixed and combined with other classes of gods. So much did this mixture pervade all the later views that some writers have seen nothing but varying forms of sun-worship in Egyptian religion. It will have been noticed however in the previous chapters what a large body of theology was entirely apart from the sun-worship, while here we treat the latter as separate from the other elements with which it was more or less combined.

Ra was the great sun-god, to whom every king pledged himself, by adopting on his accession a motto-title embodying the god's name, such as *Ra-men-kau*, ' Ra established the kas,' *Ra-sehotep-ab*, ' Ra satisfies the heart,' *Ra-neb-maat*, ' Ra is the lord of truth '; and these titles were those by which the king was best known ever after. This devotion was not primitive, but began in the fourth dynasty, and was established by the fifth dynasty being called sons of Ra, and every later king having the title ' son of Ra ' before his name. The obelisk was the emblem of Ra, and in the fifth dynasty a great obelisk temple was built in his honour at Abusir, followed also by others. Heliopolis was the centre of his worship, where Senusert I, in the twelfth dynasty, rebuilt the temple and erected the obelisks, one of which is still standing. But Ra was preceded there by another sun-god Atmu, who was the true god of the nome; and Ra, though worshipped throughout the land, was not the aboriginal god of any city. In Heliopolis he was attached to Atmu, at Thebes attached to Amen. These facts point to Ra having been introduced into Egypt by a conquering people, after the theologic settlement of the whole land. There are many suggestions that the Ra worshippers came in from Asia, and established their rule at Heliopolis. The title of the ruler of that place was the *heq*, a semitic title; and the *heq* sceptre was the sacred treasure of the temple. The ' spirits of Heliopolis ' were specially honoured, an idea more Babylonian than Egyptian. This city was a centre of literary learning and of theologic theorising which was unknown elsewhere in Egypt, but familiar in Mesopotamia. A conical stone was the embodiment of the god at Heliopolis, as in Syria. *On,* the native name of Heliopolis, occurs twice in Syria, as well as other cities named Heliopolis there in later times. The view of an early Semitic principate of Heliopolis, before the dynastic age, would unify all of these facts: and the advance of Ra worship in the fifth dynasty would be due to a revival of the influence of the eastern Delta at that time.

The form of Ra most free from admixture is that of the disk of the sun, sometimes figured between two hills at rising, sometimes between two wings, sometimes in the boat in which it floated on the celestial ocean across the sky. The winged disk has almost always two cobra serpents attached to it, and often two rams' horns; the meaning of the whole combination is that Ra protects and preserves, like the vulture brooding over its young, destroys like the cobra, and creates like the ram. This is seen by the modification where it is placed over a king's head, when the destructive cobra is omitted, and the wings are folded together as embracing and protecting the king.

This disk form is connected with the hawk-god, by being placed over the head of the hawk; and this in turn is connected with the human form by the disc resting on the hawk-headed man, which is one of the most usual types of Ra. The god is but seldom shown as being purely human, except when identified with other gods, such as Atmu, Horus, or Amon.

The worship of Ra outshone all others in the nineteenth dynasty. United to the god of Thebes as Amon Ra, he became 'king of the gods'; and the view that the soul joined Ra in his journey through the hours of the night absorbed all other views, which only became sections of this whole (see chap. xi). By the Greek times this belief seems to have largely given place to others, and it had practically vanished in the early Christian age.

Atmu (Tum) was the original god of Heliopolis and the Delta side, round to the gulf of Suez, which formerly reached up to Ismailiyeh. How far his nature as the setting sun was the result of his being identified with Ra, is not clear. It may be that he was simply a creator-god, and that the introduction of Ra led to his being unified with him. Those who take the view that the names of gods are connected with tribes, as

Set and Suti, Anuke and Anak, might well claim that Atmu or Atum belonged to the land of Aduma or Etham.

Khepera has no local importance, but is named as the morning sun. He was worshipped about the time of the nineteenth dynasty.

Aten was a conception of the sun entirely different to Ra. No human or animal form was ever attached to it; and the adoration of the physical power and action of the sun was the sole devotion. So far as we can trace, it was a worship entirely apart, and different from every other type of religion in Egypt; and the partial information that we have about it does not, so far, show a single flaw in a purely scientific conception of the source of all life and power upon earth. The Aten was the only instance of a 'jealous god' in Egypt, and this worship was exclusive of all others, and claims universality. There are traces of it shortly before Amonhotep III. He showed some devotion to it, and it was his son who took the name of Akhenaten, 'the glory of the Aten,' and tried to enforce this as the sole worship of Egypt. But it fell immediately after, and is lost in the next dynasty. The sun is represented as radiating its beams on all things, and every beam ends in a hand which imparts life and power to the king and to all else. In the hymn to the Aten the universal scope of this power is proclaimed as the source of all life and action, and every land and people are subject to it, and owe to it their existence and their allegiance. No such grand theology had ever appeared in the world before, so far as we know; and it is the forerunner of the later monotheist religions, while it is even more abstract and impersonal, and may well rank as a scientific theism.

Anher was the local god of Thinis in Upper Egypt, and Sebennytos in the Delta, a human sun-god. His name is a mere epithet, ' he who goes in heaven'; and it may well be that this was only a title of Ra, who was thus worshipped at these places.

Sopdu was the god of the eastern desert, and he was identified with the cone of glowing zodiacal light which precedes the sunrise. His emblem was a mummified hawk, or a human figure.

Nut, the embodiment of heaven, is shown as a female figure dotted over with stars. She was not worshipped nor did she belong to any one place, but was a cosmogonic idea.

Seb, the embodiment of the earth, is figured as lying on the ground while Nut bends over him. He was the 'prince of the gods,' the power that went before all the later gods, the superseded Saturn of Egyptian theology. He is rarely mentioned, and no temples were dedicated to him, but he appears in the cosmic mythology. It seems, from their positions, that very possibly Seb and Nut were the primaeval gods of the aborigines of Hottentot type, before the Osiris worshippers of European type ever entered the Nile valley.

Shu was the god of space, who lifted up Nut from off the body of Seb. He was often represented, especially in late amulets ; possibly it was believed that he would likewise raise up the body of the deceased from earth to heaven. His figure is entirely human, and he kneels on one knee with both hands lifted above his head. He was regarded as the father of Seb, the earth having been formed from space or chaos. His emblem was the ostrich feather, the lightest and most voluminous object.

Hapi, the Nile, must also be placed with Nature-gods. He is figured as a man, or two men for the Upper and Lower Niles, holding a tray of produce of the land, and having large female breasts as being the nourisher of the valley. A favourite group consists of the two Nile figures tying the plants of Upper and Lower Egypt around the

56

emblem of union. He was worshipped at Nilopolis, and also at the shrines which marked the boating stages, about a hundred in number all along the river. Festivals were held at the rising of the Nile, like those still kept up at various stages of the inundation. Hymns in honour of the river attribute all prosperity and good to its benefits.

CHAPTER VIII

BESIDES the classes of gods already described there are others who stand apart in their character, as embodying abstract ideas. Of these some are probably tribal gods; but the principle of each is so clearly marked that they must have been idealised by people who were at a relatively high level of mind. Others are frankly abstractions of artificial ideas devised in a civilised state, much like the deities Flora or the Genius of the Roman Emperor. The general inference is that these gods all belong to the latest of the peoples who contributed to the mythology, the dynastic rulers of the land.

Ptah the creator was especially worshipped at Memphis. He is figured as a mummy; and we know that full length burial and mummifying begin with the dynastic race. He was identified with the earlier animal-worship of the bull Apis;

58

but it is not likely that this originated his creative aspect, as he creates by moulding clay, or by word and will, and not by natural means. He became united with the old Memphite god of the dead, Seker, and with Osiris, as Ptah-Seker-Osiris. Thus we learn that he belonged neither to the animal worshippers, the believers in Seker, nor to the Osiride race, but to a fourth people. The compound god Ptah-Seker is shown as a bandy-legged dwarf, with wide flat head, a known aberration of growth. It seems as if we should connect this with the *pataikoi* who were worshipped by Phoenician sailors as dwarf figures, the name being similar. This points to a connection of the Phoenician race with the dynastic Egyptians. Ptah was worshipped in all ages down to Greek times.

Min was the male principle. He was worshipped mainly at Ekhmim and Koptos, and was there identified with Pan by the Greeks. He also was the god of the desert, out to the Red Sea. The oldest statues of gods are three gigantic limestone figures of Min found at Koptos; these bear relief designs of Red Sea shells and sword fish. It seems, then, that he was introduced by a people coming across from the east. His worship continued till Roman times.

Hat-hor was the female principle whose animal was the cow; and she is identified with the mother Isis. She was also identified with other earlier deities; and her forms are very numerous in different localities. There were also seven Hathors who appear as Fates, presiding over birth. Thus this goddess has a position different from any other, more generalised, more widely spread, and identified with many places and ideas. The similarity of such a position, with that of the Madonna in Italy in relation to earlier worships, suggests that the widespread devotion to her was of later introduction and superimposed on varied beliefs. The figure of Hathor sometimes has the cow's head, and often has cow's ears. The myth of Horus striking off the head of his mother Isis and replacing it by a cow's head, points to the Horus worshippers uniting Hathor with Isis. Statuettes of Hathor are not common; the head was used for an architectural capital and in the form of the sistrum, a rattle which was employed in her worship.

Maat was the goddess of truth. She is always of human form, and shown as seated holding the *ankh*, emblem of life, in her hands. She was never worshipped, and had no temples or shrines, but was represented as being offered by the kings to the gods. She also occurs in the names of several kings, and appears in the judgment scene of the weighing of the heart. She was the only idea of the older religion which was preserved by Akhenaten in his reformation; he always names himself as 'living in truth,' but as an abstraction and without the notion of any actual goddess. She is linked with Ptah, Thōth, and Ra, on different occasions.

Nefertum is a god of late times, in human form, as a youth with a lotus flower on his head. He appears to have represented growth and vegetation; and is systematised as a son of Ptah and Sekhet. No temple of his remains; but his figures, usually of bronze, are common.

Safekh was the goddess of writing. She is named in the pyramid times, and appears in scenes of the eighteenth and nineteenth dynasties.

Four pairs of elemental gods were worshipped at Hermopolis, each pair male and female; *Heh*, Eternity; *Kek*, Darkness; *Nu*, the heavenly ocean; *Nenu*, the Inundation. They are shown as human figures with the heads of frogs and serpents. There were also personifications of Seeing, Hearing, Taste, Perception, Strength, and the 'true voice' necessary to intone the magic formulae.

CHAPTER IX

BESIDES the incorporation into purely Egyptian usage of all the gods that we have noticed, there were others who always retained a foreign character. It is true that Bast, Neit, and Taurt are counted by some as foreign; but deities who are found from the pyramid times to the Roman age, and who were the patrons of capitals and of dynasties, must be counted as Egyptian; and of Taurt we do not know of any foreign source, nor should we look for any, as the hippopotamus abounded in Egypt itself.

Bēs, though figured from the eighteenth dynasty to Roman times, yet retained a foreign character. He is a dwarfish, clumsy figure, wearing a feline skin on his back, with the tail hanging down to his heels. A female figure wearing the feline skin similarly is known from the twelfth dynasty. Rarely female forms of Bēs

62

occur in late times. The source of this type is the Sudany dancer, such as may still be seen performing in Egypt, and we know that even in the fifth dynasty dancers called Denga (= Dinka tribe?) were brought as curiosities to Egypt. Bēs was often figured as dancing with a tambourine; he was the god of the dance, and protected infants from evil and witchcraft; hence he appears on the imposts of the capitals of the birth - house at Dendereh. The animal whose skin he wears is the *cynaelurus guttatus*, whose name is *bes*. Possibly Bastet, the feline goddess, was originally a female form of Bēs.

Dedun was a Nubian god, who appears to have been a creative earth-god. He was unified with Ptah, and is often named in the nineteenth dynasty.

Sati was a goddess of the cataract region, similar to Hathor, with cow's horns. She is called queen of the gods, and seems to have been the great deity of a frontier tribe.

Anqet was the goddess of the cataract island of Seheyl, and is figured wearing a high crown of feathers.

Sutekh must not be confounded with the purely Egyptian god Set or Setesh, though the two were identified. Probably they were one in

prehistoric ages; but Set was the god known
to the Egyptians, while Sutekh was the god of
the Hittites from Armenia, where he was worshipped in their home cities.

Baal was another Syrian god also identified with Set, and sometimes combined with
Mentu as a war-god in the nineteenth dynasty,
when Syrian ideas prevailed so largely in
Egypt.

Reshpu, or **Reseph**, was occasionally worshipped
as a war-god in the Syrianised age; but no
statues or temples are known to him or to
Baal.

Anta, or **Anaitis**, was a goddess of the Hittites, who appears fully armed on horseback in
the Ramesside times. Ramessu ii called his
daughter Bant-anta, 'daughter of Anta.'

Astharth, Ashtaroth, or **Astarte**, was another
Syrian goddess, who was worshipped mainly at
Memphis, where the tomb of a priestess of hers
is known. Ramessu ii named a son of his
Merastrot, 'loved of Ashtaroth.'

Qedesh, 'the holy one,' is shown as a nude
goddess standing on a lion; she may be a form
of Ashtaroth, as patroness of the *qedosheth* girls
attached to her service. The position on a lion is
a well-known one of Hittite goddesses.

THE FOREIGN GODS

Figures of foreign goddesses are often found in Egypt; they are of pottery, coarsely made, nude, and with the breasts held in the hands. They probably represent Ashtaroth.

We may also here mention some theories about the foreign connections of the Egyptian gods. The early Sumerians of Babylonia worshipped Asari, 'the strong one,' 'the prince who does good to men.' This has a strong resemblance in name and character to Asar, Osiris, of Egypt. But the connection which is proposed, from both names being written with the signs of an eye and a place, seems baseless, as the syllabic values of the signs were reversed in the two languages; either the writing or the sound of the name must be only a coincidence. Istar, another Sumerian deity, became softened in Semitic speech to Athtar, the moon-goddess of Southern Arabia; and the connection of this moon- and cow-goddess with the similar Hathor of Egypt seems very probable. Ansar was another Sumerian god, meaning 'the sky,' or the spirit world of the sky; and this might have passed into Anhar, the sky-god, known both in Upper and Lower Egypt. These connections are all with Sumerian gods, but may have been derived through their later Semitic forms. They have a general probability from the names and nature in each instance; but until we can trace some point of connection in place and in period, we can only bear these resemblances in mind as material for some larger view of early history.

CHAPTER X

MAN in all times and places has speculated on the nature and origin of the world, and connected such questions with his theology. In Egypt there are not many primitive theories of creation, though some have various elaborated forms. Of the formation of the earth there were two views. (1) That it had been brought into being by the word of a god, who when he uttered any name caused the object thereby to exist. Thōth is the principal creator by this means, and this idea probably belongs to a period soon after the age of the animal gods. (2) The other view is that Ptah framed the world as an artificer, with the aid of eight *Khnumu*, or earth-gnomes. This belongs to the theology of the abstract gods. The primitive people seem to have been content with the eternity of matter, and only personified nature when they described space (Shu) as separating the sky (Nut) from the earth (Seb). This is akin to the separation of chaos into sky and sea in Genesis.

The sun is called the egg laid by the primeval goose; and in later time this was said to be laid by a god, or modelled by Ptah. Evidently this goose egg is a primitive tale which was adapted to later theology.

The sky is said to be upheld by four pillars. These were later connected with the gods of the four quarters; but the primitive four pillars were represented together, with the capitals one over the other, in the sign *dad*, the emblem of stability. These may have belonged to the Osiris cycle, as he is 'lord of the pillars' (*daddu*), and his centre in the Delta was named Daddu from the pillars. The setting up of the pillars or *dad* emblem was a great festival in which the kings took part, and which is often represented.

The creation of life was variously attributed to different great gods where they were worshipped. Khnumu, Osiris, Amen, or Atmu, each are stated to be the creator. The mode was only defined by the theorists of Heliopolis; they imagined that Atmu self-produced Shu and Tefnut, they produced Seb and Nut, and they in turn other gods, from whom at last sprang mankind. But this is merely later theorising to fit a theology in being.

THE COSMOGONY

The cosmogonic theories, therefore, were by no means important articles of belief, but rather assumptions of what the gods were likely to have done similar to the acts of men. The creation by the word is the most elevated idea, and is parallel to the creation in Genesis.

The conception of the nature of the world was that of a great plain, over which the sun passed by day, and beneath which it travelled through the hours of night. The movement of the sun was supposed to be that of floating on the heavenly ocean, figured by its being in a boat, which was probably an expression for its flotation. The elaboration of the nature of the regions through which the sun passed at night essentially belongs to the Ra theology, and only recognises the kingdom of Osiris by placing it in one of the hours of night. The old conception of the dim realm of the cemetery-god Seker occupies the fourth and fifth hours; the sixth hour is an approach to the Osiride region, and the seventh hour is the kingdom of Osiris. Each hour was separated by gates, which were guarded by demons who needed to be controlled by magic formulae.

CHAPTER XI

THE accounts which we have of the temple ritual are of the later periods, and we must look to the buildings themselves to trace differences in the system. The oldest form of shrine was a wicker hut, with tall poles forming the sides of the door; in front of this extended an enclosure which had two poles with flags on either side of the entrance. In the middle of the enclosure or court was a staff bearing the emblem of the god. This type of shrine and open court was kept up always, and is like the Jewish type. We find stone used for the doors in the sixth dynasty, and stone-built temples in the twelfth dynasty. The earlier type of temple was essentially a resting-place for the god between the excursions of the festivals. It was open at both front and back, and a processional way led through it, so that the priests walked through, taking up the ark of the god, carrying it in procession, and then returning and depositing it again in the temple as they passed. This form lasted till the middle of the eighteenth dynasty; but the fixed shrine was already coming into use then, and seems to have become the only type after that age. This was emphasised still more in the twenty-sixth dynasty by the great monolith boxes of granite which contained not only precious statuettes, but even life-sized statues of granite. It seems that the processional form of ritual had been supplanted by the service of a more mysterious Holy of Holies.

The course of daily service by the priests was of seven parts. 1st. *Fire-making*—rubbing the fire sticks, taking the censer, putting incense in it, and lighting it. 2nd. *Opening the Shrine*—going up to the shrine, loosening the fastening, and breaking the seal, opening the door, seeing the god. 3rd. *Praise*—various prostrations, and then singing a hymn to the god. 4th. *Supplying food and incense*—offering oil and honey and incense, retiring from the shrine for a prayer, approaching and looking on the god, various prostrations, again incense, and then prayers and hymns, a figure of Maat (goddess of truth) was then presented to the god, and, lastly, more incense for all the companions of the god.

5th. *Purifying*—cleansing the figure and its shrine, and pouring out pitchers of water, and fumigating with incense. 6th. *Clothing*—dressing the god with white, green, bright red, and dark red sashes, and supplying two kinds of ointment and black and green eye paint, and scattering clean sand before him. The priest then walked four times round the shrine. 7th. *Purifying*—with incense, natron of the south and north, and two other kinds of incense. Probably such a ritual was a gradual growth of successive ages. Where a living animal was maintained as sacred, the feeding of it was a considerable service. A court was built at Memphis for the sacred Apis bull to take his exercise, and special bundles of fodder were provided. A large tank was made for the sacred crocodile in the Fayum, and the priests used to follow the reptile around the tank with the offerings brought by devotees. Similarly at Epidauros is a deep circular trench cut in the rock, with a central niche; in this a sacred serpent could be visited and fed without its being able to escape.

The priesthood was elaborated in many different kinds, and varied grades in each. There were the 'servants of the god,' who had charge of the worship and ritual; the 'pure men,' who were occupied with the acts of offerings and service; the 'divine fathers,' who had charge of the property of a god and the providing for the services; the 'reciters'; the 'female singers'; and others; and there were four grades of most of the classes.

A special divine gift was the *sa*, an essence which was imparted to the king when he knelt with his back to the god and the divine hand was placed on him. This was also imparted to a class of priests or initiated who were described as 'impregnated with the sa' of four different grades. This seems to have been a kind of ordination imparting special powers.

A fundamental idea was that the king was the priest of the land, and that all offerings (especially those for the dead) were made by him. Even though the king could not physically perform all the offerings, yet when others did so they were only acting on behalf of the priestly king of the nation. So strongly was this held that the regular formula for all offerings for the dead was 'A royal giving of offerings of such and such things for the *ka* of such an one,' or it may be rendered 'May the king give an offering.' The act itself is shown on some funeral tablets, where the king appears as making the offering,

73

while the person for whom he acts stands behind him.

Much light on the sources of the rise of the priesthood is given by the titles borne by the priests of the various capitals of the provinces or nomes. Many of these refer to what were purely secular occupations in later times, and we thus learn that the priestly character was attached to the principal person, be he king, or leader in other ways. In one city it was the King and His Loved Son who were the priests, in another it was the General, in another the Warrior who became the priest; elsewhere it was the Great Constructor, in another city the Great Commander of Workmen; one city raised the Manager of the Inundation to the priesthood, and very naturally the Great Physician or medicine man became priest in another place. The Eldest Son was the title of another priesthood, much as the later kings made their eldest son high priest. A very curious view of the priestess preceding the establishment of a priest is given by some cities; one where she was called the Nurse, and the priest was the Youth, and another city names the priestess the 'Appeaser of the Spirit' and the priest the 'Favourite Child.'

Purely religious functions are only a minority

of the priestly titles in the Delta, such as the Seer, the Great Seer, the Chief of the Feast, and the Opener of the Mouth, referring to enabling the statue of the god to speak, or opening the mouth of the mummy to enable it to live. A full analysis of the priestly titles would give a picture of the society in which priesthood arose, but it is a subject which has not been systematically studied.

CHAPTER XII

In the latest age of ancient Egypt the religious writings were largely translated into Greek, at a time when they were studied and collected as embodying the ideas of a world which was already fading away. This venerated past kept its hold on the imagination as containing mystic powers of compelling the unseen, and strange travesties of ancient formulae, the efficacy of which could not be rivalled by any later writings which were baldly intelligible. There were four main classes of writings, on theology, ritual, science, and medicine. Though the late compilations have almost entirely perished, yet we can gather their nature from the portions of the original documents which are preserved from earlier times.

The most popular work in the later dynasties was that which has been called the *Book of the Dead* by modern writers. We must not conceive of it as a bound up whole, like our Bible; but rather as an incongruous accumulation of charms and formulae, parts of which were taken at discretion by various scribes according to local or individual tastes. No single papyrus contains even the greater part of it, and the choice made among the heterogeneous material is infinitely varied. The different sections have been numbered by modern editors, starting with the order found in some of the best examples, and more than two hundred such chapters are recognised. Every variety of belief finds place in this large collection; every charm or direction which could benefit the dead found a footing here if it attained popularity. From prehistoric days downward it formed a religious repertory without limits or regulation. Portions known in the close of the old kingdom entirely vanish in later copies, while others appear which are obviously late in origin. The incessant adding of notes, incorporation of glosses, and piling of explanations one on the other, has increased the confusion. And to add to our bewilderment, the scribes were usually quite callous about errors in a writing which was never to be seen or used by living eyes; and the corruptions, which have been in turn made worse, have left hardly any sense in many parts. At

RELIGION OF ANCIENT EGYPT

best it is difficult to follow the illusions of a lost faith, but amid all the varieties of idea and bad readings superposed, the task of critical understanding is almost hopeless. The full study of such a work will need many new discoveries and occupy generations of critical ingenuity. We can distinguish certain groups of chapters, an Osirian section on the kingdom of Osiris and the service of it, a theological section, a set of incantations, formulae for the restoration of the heart, for the protection of the soul from spirits and serpents in the hours of night, charms to escape from perils ordained by the gods, an account of the paradise of Osiris, a different version of the kingdom and judgment of Osiris, a Heliopolitan doctrine about the *ba*, and its powers of transformation entirely apart from all that is stated elsewhere, the account of the re-union of soul and body, magic formulae for entering the Osirian kingdom, another account of the judgment of Osiris, charms for the preservation of the mummy and for making efficacious amulets, together with various portions of popular beliefs.

In contrast to the mainly Osirian character above described, we see the solar religion dominant in the *Book of Am Duat,* or that which is in the underworld. This describes the successive hours of the night, each hour fenced off with gates which are guarded by monsters. At each gate the right spells must be uttered to subdue the evil powers, and so pass through with the sun. The older beliefs in Seker, the god of the silent land, and Osiris, the king of the blessed world, are fitted in to the newer system by allotting some hours to these other realms as a part of the solar journey. A variant of this work is the *Book of Gates*, describing the gates of the hours, but omitting Seker and making Osiris more important. These books represent the fashionable doctrines of the kings in the Ramesside times, and are mainly known from the royal tombs on which they are inscribed.

Another branch of the sacred books survives in the formal theology of the schools which grouped gods together in trinities or enneads. These were certainly very ancient, having been formed under the Heliopolitan supremacy before the rise of the first dynasty. And if the artificial co-ordinating of the gods of varied sources is thus ancient, we have a glimpse of the much greater age of the Osiride gods, and still further of the primitive gods Seb and Nut, and the earliest worship of animals.

The great ennead of Heliopolis consisted of Shu, Tefnut, Seb, Nut, Osiris, Isis, Set, Nebhat, and Horus; there were also secondary and tertiary enneads of lesser gods. When the sun-god Atmu became prominent, Horus was omitted and the eight other gods were called children of Atmu, who headed the group, as in the Pyramid texts. The nine are not composed of three triads, but of four pairs and a leader. This is on the same type as the four pairs of elemental gods at Hermopolis under the chief god Tahuti. The triads were usual at most cities, but were in many cases clearly of artificial arrangement, in order to follow a type, the deities being of very unequal importance. At Thebes, Amon, Mut, and Khonsu; at Memphis, Ptah, Sekhet, and the deified man Imhotep; and in general Osiris, Isis, and Horus, were the principal triads.

CHAPTER XIII

A PEOPLE so deeply imbued with religious ideas as the Egyptians doubtless carried their habits of worship beyond the temple gates. But unfortunately we have no graphic or connected view of their private devotions. At the present day a few natives will scrupulously follow the daily ritual of Islam; many keep up some convenient portion, such as the religious aspect of an evening bath after the day's work; but most of the peasantry have little or no religious observances. Perhaps the average of mankind does not differ very greatly, in various countries, in its extent of religious observance: and most likely the ancient Egyptian varied in usages much like the modern.

The funeral offerings for the deceased ancestors certainly filled a large place in observances; the drink offerings poured out upon the altar in the

F   81

chapel, and the cakes brought for the *ka* to feed upon, were the lmain expression of family piety. How serious were such services is seen by their expansion into endowments for great tombs, extending to the great temples and priesthoods for the kings. The eldest son was the sacrificing priest for his progenitors, as in China and India at present; he was called the *an-mut-f*, or 'support of his mother,' and is figured as leading the worship in the adoration of deceased kings. But all the sons took part in the sacrifices, and trapped the birds (*Medum*, x, xiii), or slaughtered the ox for the *ka* of their father. Such family sacrifices were the occasions of social feasts and family reunions; of later times the remains of the feasts were found strewing the cemetery at Hawara in the tomb chapels; and to this day both Copts and Mohammedans hold family feasts and spend the night at the tombs of their ancestors.

All offerings were considered to be presented only by the king, as the great high-priest of all the land. Every formula of offering began ' May the king give an offering '; and the figure of the king making the offering, while the offerer stands behind him, is actually shown as late as the eighteenth dynasty.

PRIVATE WORSHIP

The primitive belief in the tree-goddess, the Hathor who dwelt in the thick sycomore tree, and showered sycomore figs abundantly on her devotees, was a popular worship. It was by no means bound up with the tomb service, as in one case a red recess in a dwelling room had a panel picture at the top of it showing the tree goddess giving blessings to her worshipper (*Ramesseum*, xx).

The latter instance gives the meaning of a curious domestic feature in the well-to-do houses of the bureaucracy at Tell-el-Amarna. In the central hall of the house was a recess in the wall painted bright red. It varied from twenty-three to fifty-one inches wide, and was at least five or six feet high. Sometimes there is an inner recess in the middle twenty-five to thirty-three inches wide. From the religious scene over such a recess it seems that these were the foci for family worship.

The abundance of little statuettes of gods of glazed pottery, and often of bronze, silver, and even of gold, show how common was the custom of wearing such devotional objects. Children especially wore figures of Bes, and less commonly Taurt, the protecting genii of childhood.

Another feature of popular religion was the

harvest festival. The grain was heaped, the winnowing shovels and rakes stuck upright in it, and then holding up the boards (which were used to scrape up the grain) in each hand, adoration was paid to Rannut, the serpent-goddess of the harvest.

The observance of lucky and unlucky days was prevalent. The fragment of a calendar shows each day marked good or evil, or triply good or evil.

The household amulets in the prehistoric days were the great serpent stones with figures of the coiled serpent; much suggesting an earlier use of large ammonites. In later times the image of Horus subduing the powers of evil seems to have been the protective figure of the house.

When we reach Roman times we have a fuller view of the popular worship in the terra-cotta figures. At Ehnasya, for instance, we find the following proportions—five of Serapis, five Isis, twenty-four Horus, four Bes, one goddess of palm trees. It was especially the worship of Horus that was developed in this line. The kind of shrines used in the houses are also shown by the terracottas. These were wooden framed cupboards, with doors below, over them a recess between two pillars to hold the image, and a lamp burning before it, and the whole crowned with a cornice of uræi. Smaller little lamp holders were also made to hang up, and very possibly to place with a lamp on a grave. At present mud hutches are made to place lamps in on holy sites in Egypt.

The terra-cottas have also preserved the forms of the wayside shrines. These were certainly influenced in their architecture by Greek models, but the idea is probably much older. The shrines were sometimes a little chamber, with a domed top, like a modern *wely* or saint's tomb, or sometimes a roof on four pillars with a dwarf wall or lattice work around three sides. Such were the places for wayside devotions and passing prayers, as among the Egyptians of the present day.

CHAPTER XIV

FORTUNATELY we have preserved to us a considerable body of the maxims of conduct from the Pyramid times; and these show very practically what were the ideals and the motives of the early people. This is only a small side of the present subject, but it will be found fully stated in *Religion and Conscience in Ancient Egypt.*

The repudiation of sins before the judgment of Osiris is the earliest code of morals, and it is striking that in this there are no family duties. Such an exclusion points to the family being unimportant in early times, the matriarchate perhaps then excluding the responsibility of the man. In the earliest form the prominence of duties is in the order of those to equals, to inferiors, to gods, and to the man's own character. In later times the duties to inferiors have almost vanished, and the inner duties to character are

86

greatly extended, being felt to lie at the root of
all else.

The ideal character was drawn in the maxims
as being strong, steadfast, commanding, direct,
self-respecting, avoiding inferior companionships,
active, and above all truthful and straightforward.
Discretion, quietness, and reserve were enforced,
and a dignified endurance without pride was to
be attained.

In material things energy and self-reliance were
held up, and a judicious respect for, and imitation
of, successful men. Covetousness was specially
reprobated, and luxury and self-indulgence were
looked on as a course which ends in bitterness.

The aspect of marriage depended essentially on
property. Where a woman had property of her
own she was mistress of the house, and her
husband was but a kind of permanent boarder.
Though in early times, and among the priestesses
later, the choice by a woman was scarcely regarded as permanent. Where, however, the
household depended on the work of the man, he
naturally took the leading part. But the code
of abstract morality, and the dictates of common
prudence, between men and women, were of as
high a standard as in any ancient or modern
peoples. No reasonable legislator would wish to

add more, although six thousand years and Christianity have intervened since the Egyptian framed his life. The family sense of duty in training and advancing a man's sons was strongly urged.

In the general interchange of social life perhaps the main feature was that of consideration for others. A higher standard of good feeling and kindliness existed than any that we know of among ancient peoples, or among most modern nations. The council-hall of the local ruler was the main theatre for ability; and the injunctions to be fearless, and at the same time gentle and cautious, would improve the character of any modern assembly. The greater number of precepts however relate to the judicious conduct toward inferiors. Justice and good discipline were the necessary basis, but they were to be always tempered by respect for the feelings and comfort of the servants.

The religious aspect of ethics was almost confined to the respect for the property and offerings of the gods. But the more spiritual side was touched in the precept, 'That which is detestable in the sanctuary of god are noisy feasts; if thou implore him with a loving heart, of which all the words are mysterious, he will do thy

88

matters, he hears thy words, he accepts thine offerings.'

The permanence of the Egyptian character will strike any one who knows the modern native. The essential mode of justification in the judgment was by the declaration of the deceased that he had not done various crimes; and to this day the Egyptian will rely on justifying himself by sheer assertion that he has not done wrong, in face of absolute proofs to the contrary. The main fault of character that was condemned was covetousness, and it is the feeling which wrecks the possibility of Egyptian independence at present. The intrusion of scheming underlings between the master and his men is noted as a failing; and exactly this trouble continually occurs now, when every servant tries to turn his position to an advantage over those who do business with his master. The dominance of the scribe in managing affairs and making profits was familiar in ancient as in modern times. And recent events in Egypt have reminded us of the old fickleness shown in the saying, ' Thy entering into a village begins with acclamations; at thy going out thou art saved by thy hand.'

CHAPTER XV

How far Egypt in its earlier days had influenced the faiths of other countries we cannot trace, owing to our ignorance of the early civilisations of the world. But in the later times the extension of the popular religion of Egypt can only be paralleled by the spread of Christianity or Islam. Isis was worshipped in Greece in the fourth century B.C., and in Italy in the second century. Soon after she won her way into official recognition by Sulla, and immediately after the death of Julius a temple to Isis was actually erected by the government. Once firmly established in Rome, the spread of Imperial power carried her worship over the world; emperors became her priests, and the humble centurion in remote camps honoured her in the wilds of France, Germany, Yorkshire, or the Sahara.

Not only Isis but also Osiris claimed the world's

worship. In the new form of the Osir-hapi of Memphis, or Serapis, the Ptolemies identified him with Zeus, both in appearance and by attributes. And, by the time of Nero, Isis and Osiris were said to be the deities of all the world. An interesting outline of this subject will be found in Professor Dill's *Roman Society from Nero to Aurelius*.

Besides these parent gods their son Horus also conquered the world with them. Isis and Horus, the Queen of Heaven and the Holy Child, became the popular deities of the later age of Egypt, and their figures far outnumber those of all other gods. Horus in every form of infancy was the loved *bambino* of the Egyptian women. Again Horus appears carried on the arm of his mother in a form which is indistinguishable from that adopted by Christianity soon after.

We see, then, throughout the Roman world the popular worship of the Queen of Heaven, *Mater Dolorosa*, Mother of God, patroness of sailors, and her infant son Horus the child, the benefactor of men, who took captive all the powers of evil. And this worship spread and increased in Egypt and elsewhere until the growing power of Christianity compelled a change. The old worship continued; for the Syrian maid became transformed into an entirely different figure, Queen of Heaven, Mother of God, patroness of sailors, occupying the position and attributes already belonging to the world-wide goddess; and the Divine Teacher, the Man of Sorrows, became transformed into the entirely different figure of the Potent Child. Isis and Horus still ruled the affections and worship of Europe with a change of names.

Egypt also exercised an immense influence upon the Church in the Trinitarian controversy. That was a purely Egyptian dispute, between two presbyters brought up in the atmosphere of intricacies about the *ka*, the *khu*, the *khat*, the *ba*, the *sahu*, the *khaybat*, and the various other entities which constituted man. To carry forward similar refinements concerning the Divine Nature was as congenial to such minds as it was incomprehensible to the Western. And the dispute finally rested on the question of whether ‘before time’ was the same as ‘from eternity.’ Such was the struggle which Arius and Athanasius thrust upon the Church; a dispute which would never have been heard of in such a shape but for their Egyptian origin.

In another direction Egypt was also dominant. From some source—perhaps the Buddhist mission

THE INFLUENCE OF EGYPT

of Asoka—the ascetic life of recluses was established in the Ptolemaic times, and monks of the Serapeum illustrated an ideal to man which had been as yet unknown in the West. This system of monasticism continued, until Pachomios, a monk of Serapis in Upper Egypt, became the first Christian monk in the reign of Constantine. Quickly imitated in Syria, Asia Minor, Gaul, and other provinces, as well as in Italy itself, the system passed into a fundamental position in mediaeval Christianity, and the reverence of mankind has been for fifteen hundred years bestowed on an Egyptian institution.

We thus see how the religious ideas of six thousand years or more have still survived and continued their power over civilised man, renamed but scarcely changed; and it is shown how new religious ideas can but transform, but not eradicate, the ancestral beliefs of past ages.

INDEX

INDEX

Buto, 42.
Byblos, Osiris's coffin at, 39.

COMPOUND NAMES OF GODS, 28.
Cobra, 25.
Crocodile, 25.

Dad, 68.
Dedun, 63.
Demons, 5.
Dendereh, 63.

EARTH, creation of, 67.
Edfu, hawk-worship, 24, 45.
Ekhmim, 59.
Eldest son offers to ancestors, 82.
Entities, two vitalise the body, 8.
Eye of Horus, 46.

FATES, seven Hat-hors, 60.
Fayum, crocodile worship, 25, 72.
Fish worship, 26.
Frog, Heqt, 34.
Future life, 12.

GOD, Christian view of, 5.
—— Hebrew view of, 5.
—— jealous, 5, 54.
—— view of, held by Islam, 5.
Gods, Chinese views of, 3.
—— communications from, 3.
—— divine, merged in human, 3.
—— great gods, 3, 5.
—— grouped owing to political
      unions, 5.
—— misunderstanding of, 1.
—— mortality of, 2.
—— non-existence of other, 5.
—— offerings to, 2.
—— one to a city, 4.
—— profusion of, 3.
—— Siberian views of, 3.

Gods, suffering of, 2.
—— Sumerian views of, 3, 65.
—— Turanian views of, 3, 4.
—— wife of, 2.

HARMAKHIS, 46.
Hat-hor, 60.
—— cow, 23.
—— Sinai temple, 22.
—— tree goddess, 13, 83.
Hati, the physical heart, 9.
Hapi, 56.
—— bull, 23.
Hawk, 24.
Heart, weighed against feather,
      14.
Heh, 61.
Heqt, 34.
Heliopolis, associated with Ra,18,
      51, 52.
Hermopolis, 32, 61.
Hershefi, ram, 23, 34.
Heru. *See* Horus.
Hierakonpolis, boats, 18.
—— hawk-worship, 24, 45.
Hippopotamus, 24.
Hittite god Sutekh akin to Set,
      64.
—— goddess Anta, 64.
Horus, 35, 44, 91.
—— hawk, 24.
—— overcomes noxious creatures,
      27, 46.
—— Ra's eyes obtained for, 10.
—— a self-existent god, 4.
—— stands on *nub*, 46.
—— supersedes Set, 34.
Hyksos, 42.

IBIS, Tahuti, 25.
Ichneumon, 24.
Immortality Egyptian belief in,7.

INDEX

INDEX

INDEX

Printed by T. and A. CONSTABLE, Printers to His Majesty
at the Edinburgh University Press

www.ingramcontent.com/pod-product-compliance
Ingram Content Group UK Ltd.
Pitfield, Milton Keynes, MK11 3LW, UK
UKHW042150280225
455719UK00001B/251

9 781108 065788